GRIZZLY BEAR

Dylanna Press

Meet the Grizzly Bear

Grizzly bears are one of the largest and most powerful land predators in North America. They roam forests, mountains, and river valleys, mainly in Alaska, western Canada, and parts of the northwestern United States. With their thick fur, massive paws, and long claws, they are built for strength and survival.

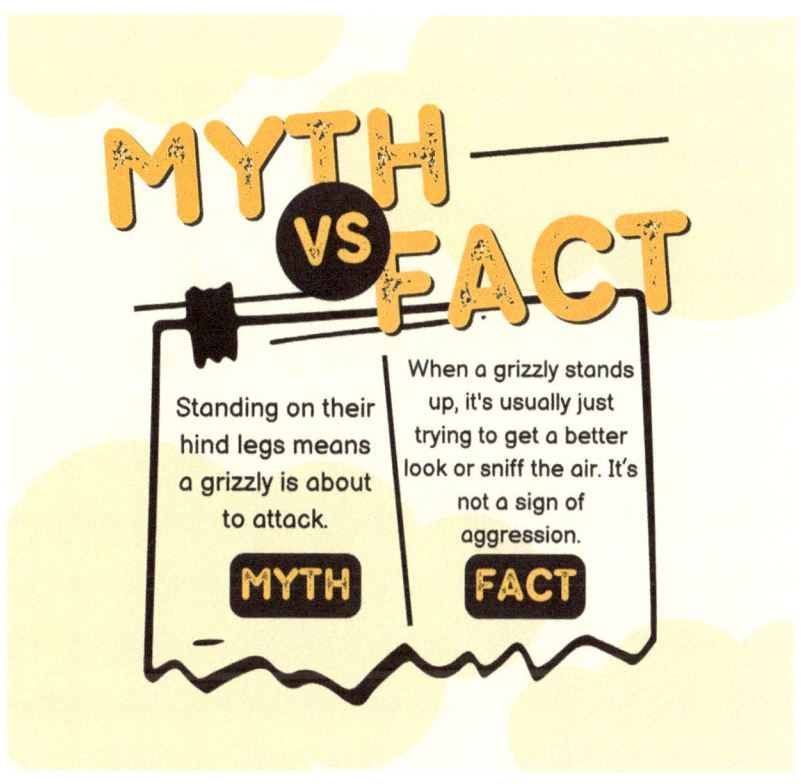

Historically, grizzly bears lived across much of North America, from the Great Plains to Mexico. But as human populations expanded, their numbers declined. Today, most wild grizzlies live in protected areas like Yellowstone National Park and remote wilderness regions.

Grizzly bears (*Ursus arctos horribilis*) are a subspecies of the brown bear (*Ursus arctos*), closely related to European and Siberian brown bears. They belong to the *Ursidae* family, which includes black bears, polar bears, and giant pandas.

For thousands of years, grizzly bears have been important to Indigenous cultures, folklore, and ecosystems. Scientists continue to study these incredible animals to better understand their intelligence, behaviors, and role in nature.

What Do Grizzly Bears Look Like?

Grizzly bears are some of the most powerful mammals on land. Adult grizzlies can stand 6 to 8 feet (1.8 to 2.4 meters) tall on their hind legs, and on all fours they usually measure 3 to 4.5 feet (0.9 to 1.4 meters) at the shoulder. Males are much larger than females, weighing between 400 to 900 pounds (180 to 408 kg), while females are typically 250 to 600 pounds (113 to 272 kg).

Their thick, shaggy fur helps them stay warm in harsh mountain climates. The fur color can range from light blond to deep brown or even black, and many grizzlies have silver-tipped hairs on their backs and shoulders, giving them their distinctive "grizzled" look.

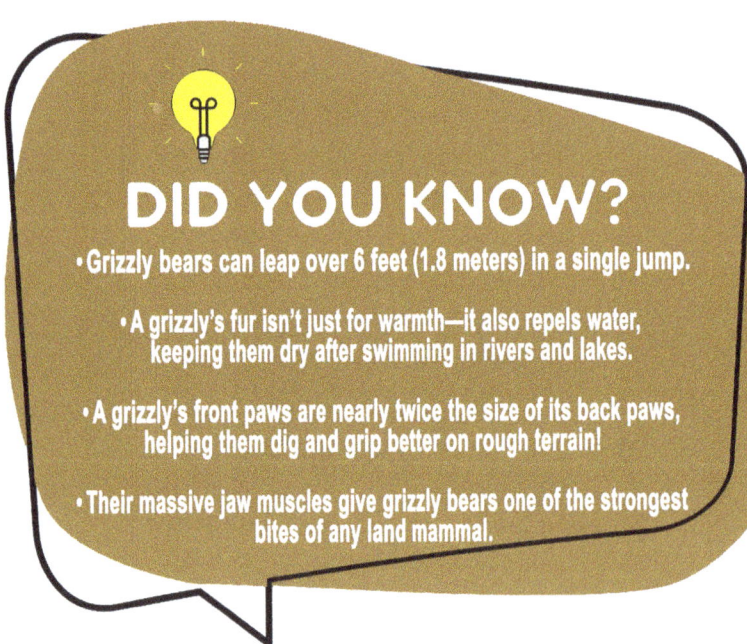

DID YOU KNOW?
- Grizzly bears can leap over 6 feet (1.8 meters) in a single jump.
- A grizzly's fur isn't just for warmth—it also repels water, keeping them dry after swimming in rivers and lakes.
- A grizzly's front paws are nearly twice the size of its back paws, helping them dig and grip better on rough terrain!
- Their massive jaw muscles give grizzly bears one of the strongest bites of any land mammal.

One of the most recognizable features of a grizzly bear is the large hump on its shoulders. This hump is pure muscle, making grizzlies incredibly strong. They use this power for digging, tearing into logs, and overpowering prey.

Their massive paws and long, curved claws—growing up to 4 inches (10 cm) long—are perfectly designed for digging dens, flipping over rocks, and catching prey. Though their claws aren't great for climbing trees, they make grizzlies formidable hunters and foragers. With a single swipe, a grizzly's powerful front paw can break bones or knock over a large animal.

Despite their size, grizzly bears are fast and agile. They can run up to 35 mph (56 km/h)—faster than a galloping horse over short distances! They're also strong swimmers, capable of crossing wide rivers, and they navigate steep, rugged terrain with ease.

Grizzlies rely on their sharp senses to survive. Their eyesight is similar to a human's, and they can detect movement from a distance. Their hearing is excellent, allowing them to pick up distant sounds in their environment. Most impressive of all is their sense of smell, which is seven times stronger than a bloodhound's. Grizzlies can detect food, other animals, or danger from miles away, making their noses one of their greatest survival tools.

Where Do Grizzlies Live?

Grizzly bears can live in many different places. They're very adaptable! Historically, they lived across much of North America, from coastal areas to open prairies and mountain forests. Today, they're mostly found in Alaska, western Canada, and parts of the northwestern United States.

These versatile bears live in several types of homes. In coastal areas, they visit river valleys where they can catch salmon. In mountains, they travel between different heights with the seasons. They go to lower valleys in spring for early plants and climb to mountain meadows in summer for berries and roots.

QUESTION
Do grizzly bears live in the same place all year?

ANSWER
Not usually! Grizzlies move with the seasons, following food sources.

Forests are important for grizzlies, giving them shelter, places to make winter dens, and food like berries and nuts. Open meadows are good places to dig for roots and hunt for ground squirrels.

An adult grizzly needs a lot of space to find everything it needs. Males have larger territories than females. Some male grizzlies roam over areas as large as 1,000 square miles (2,600 square kilometers)!

Water is vital for grizzlies. They are excellent swimmers and often live near streams, rivers, and lakes. These water sources provide food like fish, fresh drinking water, and places to cool off during hot summer days.

Grizzlies move with the seasons, going where food is available. They follow spring plants up mountain slopes, look for ripe berries in summer, and move to lower areas in fall to prepare for winter hibernation.

Grizzly bears have several amazing physical **adaptations** that help them survive in their environments.

- **Muscle Power:** One of the most noticeable features of a grizzly bear is the large hump on its shoulders. This hump is made of muscle and gives the bear powerful strength for digging, climbing, and tearing into logs or prey. It also helps support their front legs, which do most of the work when foraging and hunting.

- **Powerful Claws:** Grizzlies have long, curved claws that can be up to 4 inches (10 cm) long. These claws are perfect tools for digging up roots, ripping apart rotten logs for insects, and catching slippery fish. Though they aren't built for climbing trees like black bear claws, they're ideal for life on the ground.

- **Strong Jaws and Teeth:** Grizzly bears have a combination of sharp front teeth for slicing and flat molars for grinding. Their strong jaw muscles allow them to eat a wide variety of foods—from tough plant roots to meat and bone.

- **Super Senses:** A grizzly's sense of smell is one of the strongest in the animal kingdom. They can detect scents from miles away, including food, other bears, or potential threats. Their hearing is also excellent.

- **Winter-Ready Coat:** Grizzlies have dense fur and a thick layer of body fat that protect them from cold temperatures. These layers act like insulation, keeping them warm even during snowy winters or while sleeping in their dens.

- **Seasonal Adaptability:** Grizzlies are masters of seasonal living. In the spring and summer, they build up fat by eating as much as they can. In the fall, their bodies prepare for hibernation by slowing down metabolism. During winter, their thick fur and stored fat allow them to sleep for months without eating.

- **Padded Feet:** Despite their size, grizzlies can move quietly due to the soft pads on their feet, which help them walk silently through forests. Their wide paws also give them traction on loose soil, rocky slopes, and snowy ground.

Thanks to these incredible adaptations, grizzly bears can survive in some of the wildest and most challenging environments in North America. They are strong, smart, and built for life on the move.

---

adaptations – special body parts or behaviors that help animals survive in their environment

What Do Grizzly Bears Eat?

Grizzly bears are some of the most versatile eaters in the animal world. These large mammals are omnivores, meaning they eat both plants and animals. Depending on the season and where they live, grizzlies may eat berries, roots, fish, insects, small mammals, carrion, and even grass. In fact, plants make up most of a grizzly's diet!

During spring, grizzlies wake up from hibernation hungry and begin foraging for fresh grass, roots, and bulbs. As the weather warms, they add insects and small animals to their menu. Summer and early fall are the most important times for feeding—grizzlies eat nearly nonstop to build up fat for winter. This is when they find berries, nuts, and fish, especially salmon in coastal and river regions. In a single day, a grizzly can eat over 90 pounds (41 kg) of food!

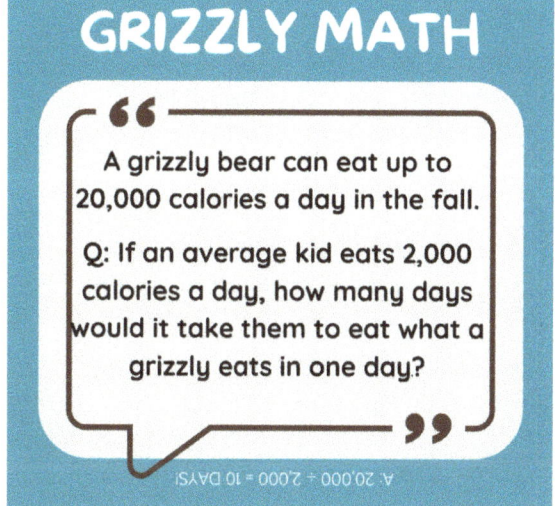

GRIZZLY MATH

" A grizzly bear can eat up to 20,000 calories a day in the fall.

Q: If an average kid eats 2,000 calories a day, how many days would it take them to eat what a grizzly eats in one day? "

A: 20,000 ÷ 2,000 = 10 DAYS!

Grizzly bears are skilled hunters and foragers. They'll flip over logs and rocks to find insects, dig into hillsides for roots, and use their sharp sense of smell to locate carcasses from miles away. In places with salmon runs, grizzlies become expert fishers, using their paws and jaws to catch slippery fish right out of the water.

Grizzlies also scavenge, feeding on animals that have already died. This helps clean up the environment and prevents the spread of disease—a vital role in their ecosystems. Though they can hunt, grizzlies rarely chase large animals unless food is scarce.

Their teeth and digestive systems are perfectly suited to this varied diet. They have sharp front teeth for slicing and broad back molars for grinding plants. Like other omnivores, their stomachs are strong but simple, breaking down everything from raw meat to tough plant fibers.

Grizzlies need large amounts of food to survive the winter months. In fall, they go into a feeding frenzy called hyperphagia, during which they eat nearly all day long to build up the thick layer of fat they'll need for hibernation.

Thanks to their flexible diet and strong foraging skills, grizzly bears can survive in all kinds of environments and changing conditions. They're not picky eaters—they're survivors.

Life on Their Own

Grizzly bears are mostly solitary animals, meaning they spend most of their lives alone. Unlike animals that live in herds or packs, grizzlies prefer to roam, hunt, and sleep by themselves. But that doesn't mean they're completely anti-social—grizzlies do interact with one another, especially when food is plentiful or during mating season.

Female grizzlies, called sows, are the most social of all. They stay with their cubs for up to two to three years, teaching them how to find food, stay safe, and explore their surroundings. Mothers are very protective and will fiercely defend their young from threats—even from other bears.

Male grizzlies, or boars, usually live alone. They roam over larger areas than females and sometimes cross paths with other males. These encounters can lead to growls, bluff charges, or even fights—especially if there's competition for food or a female.

DID YOU KNOW?
- Grizzly bears sometimes leave claw marks on trees to mark their territory and show how big they are.
- Grizzlies can go weeks or even months without seeing another bear, especially in remote wilderness areas.
- During salmon season, dozens of grizzlies may feed along the same river, each keeping their distance to avoid fights.

In places with lots of food, like salmon streams or berry patches, multiple bears may feed in the same area. Grizzlies use body language—like standing tall, huffing, or swaying—and scent marks to communicate with other bears and avoid conflict. Larger or more dominant bears usually get first pick, while smaller bears keep their distance and wait their turn.

Grizzlies also use sounds to express themselves—like huffs, moans, growls, and roars. They communicate with posture, too: standing tall, lowering their heads, or swaying from side to side to show how they feel.

Young grizzlies, especially cubs and yearlings, are curious and playful. They wrestle, chase, and climb, all while building the skills they'll need to survive on their own. As they grow older, they begin spending more time alone, eventually leaving their mother to live independently.

Even though they don't live in permanent groups, grizzlies recognize other bears by scent and memory. They may even avoid trails where a more dominant bear has recently passed, using their sharp noses to stay out of trouble.

On the Move

Grizzly bears are great wanderers, often covering dozens of miles in search of food, mates, or a place to hibernate. Each bear has a home range—an area it regularly travels—but these ranges can be huge, especially for adult males. A single grizzly's range might be as large as 500 to 1,500 square miles (1,300 to 3,900 square km)!

Unlike animals with fixed **territories**, grizzlies don't usually defend their home ranges. Instead, they follow seasonal patterns, returning to favorite feeding grounds like berry patches, salmon streams, and meadows at just the right time. Their incredible memory and sense of smell help them remember where and when food is most abundant.

Grizzlies don't migrate in large groups, but they are always on the move. In the spring, they descend from mountain dens to lower elevations where plants start growing first. In summer and fall, they may travel far and wide to find high-calorie foods like nuts, roots, and fish before winter.

Grizzlies usually walk at a calm, steady pace but they can cover long distances in a single day. Their strong limbs and padded feet make it easy for them to move through forests, over mountains, across rivers, and even through snow. When needed, they can run up to 35 miles per hour (56 km/h) for short bursts—fast enough to catch prey or escape danger.

As they travel, grizzlies leave signs behind: scratches on trees, rubbed bark, dug-up soil, and scent markings. These clues help other bears know who's been there and may help avoid dangerous encounters.

Today, some grizzly populations are limited by roads, fences, and human development, which can cut off access to traditional feeding or denning areas. To help, scientists and conservationists are working to create **wildlife corridors** that connect safe habitats, allowing bears to roam freely across the landscape.

---

territory – an area that an animal considers its home and sometimes defends from others of the same kind

wildlife corridor – a protected pathway that allows animals to move safely between different areas

A Day in the Life

Grizzly bears follow a daily rhythm that shifts with the seasons. Their activities revolve around finding food, conserving energy, and staying alert. Because they live in a wide range of environments, a grizzly's routine can look very different depending on the time of year and the availability of food. During spring, summer, and fall, grizzlies are most active in the early morning and late evening, especially during hot weather. In cooler seasons or in northern regions, they may be active throughout the day.

A typical day begins at sunrise, as the bear wakes up and sniffs the air for nearby food sources. It may start the day by digging for roots, flipping over rocks for insects, or heading to a riverbank to fish for salmon. Grizzlies are opportunistic eaters—they'll snack on berries, carrion, grasses, or even small animals, depending on what's available.

By midmorning, a grizzly might take a break, especially after a large meal. They often rest in shaded spots, beds of tall grass, or dug-out hollows, where they can cool down and stay hidden. These rest periods may last just a few minutes or stretch into long, peaceful naps.

As the day continues, the bear may travel across meadows, forests, or rivers, following well-worn paths to familiar feeding sites. If food is abundant—like during salmon season or berry peak—they may spend hours in one spot, eating as much as possible. In fall, when they prepare for hibernation, grizzlies enter a phase called hyperphagia, eating almost nonstop to build up fat reserves.

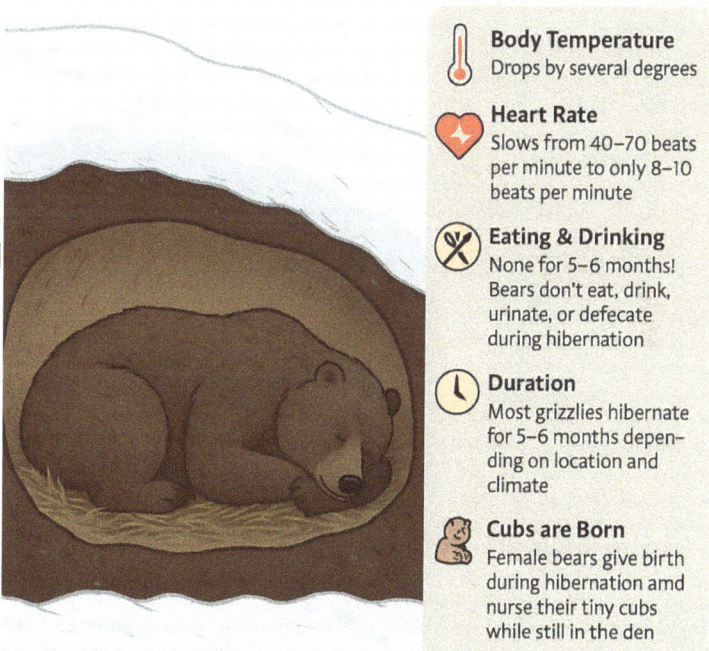

Inside a Grizzly's Winter Den

Body Temperature
Drops by several degrees

Heart Rate
Slows from 40–70 beats per minute to only 8–10 beats per minute

Eating & Drinking
None for 5–6 months! Bears don't eat, drink, urinate, or defecate during hibernation

Duration
Most grizzlies hibernate for 5–6 months depending on location and climate

Cubs are Born
Female bears give birth during hibernation amd nurse their tiny cubs while still in the den

Evening brings cooler temperatures and another chance to forage before dark. Grizzlies can see fairly well in low light, but they mostly rely on their powerful sense of smell and hearing to find food after dark. Others may settle into a sheltered area for rest. Grizzlies don't sleep deeply like humans unless they're hibernating. They're light sleepers and always alert to sounds or smells around them. Their days are shaped by survival: eat, rest, stay aware, and be ready to move.

In winter, life changes dramatically. Grizzlies retreat to dens they've dug into hillsides or beneath tree roots. There, they hibernate for several months, surviving on stored body fat. Their heart rate and breathing slow, and they won't eat, drink, or go to the bathroom the entire time.

Mating and Birth

Grizzly bears mate once a year, usually between May and July, when both males and females are most active. During this time, males roam long distances in search of females that are ready to mate.

Male grizzlies may compete for the chance to mate, sometimes following a female for days and even confronting rival males. While fights do happen, many competitions are decided through size, strength, and displays of dominance—such as standing tall, swaying, or bluff-charging. After mating, the male does not stay to help raise the young.

One of the most amazing things about grizzly reproduction is delayed implantation. After mating, the fertilized eggs develop to a certain point and then stop growing. They stay in a resting state inside the mother's body for several months. This special adaptation allows the female's body to check if she has enough fat reserves before committing to a pregnancy.

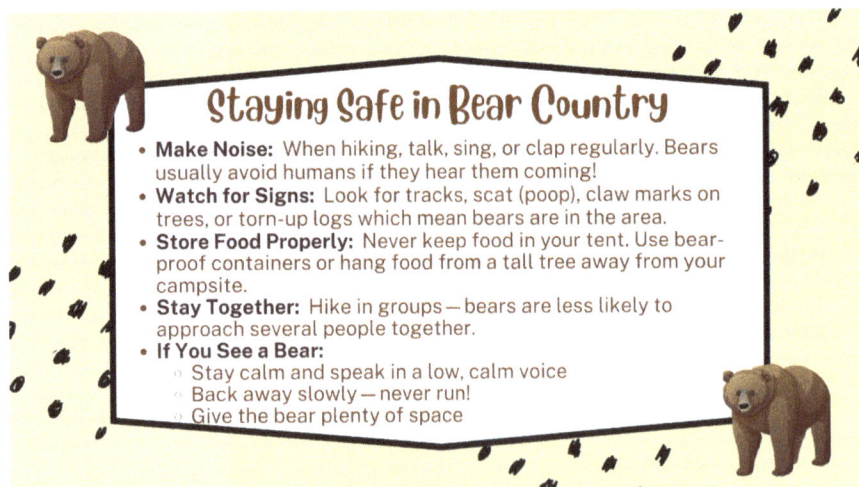

If the female has gained enough fat by fall to support herself and her cubs through hibernation, the eggs will attach to the uterine wall around November, and active pregnancy begins. If she hasn't stored enough fat, the embryos might be reabsorbed. This ensures that cubs are born when conditions are best for their survival.

Female grizzlies give birth in their winter dens, usually in January or February. Cubs are born tiny, blind, and nearly hairless, weighing only about one pound (0.5 kg)—smaller than a squirrel! Most litters have two cubs, though single cubs and triplets sometimes happen. Quadruplets are extremely rare.

A grizzly bear's total pregnancy—including delayed implantation—lasts about 6 to 8 months, but the actual development of the cubs takes only the final 2 months.

Because grizzly cubs stay with their mother for several years, females usually give birth only once every 3 to 4 years. This slow reproduction rate is one reason protecting adult females is so important for grizzly populations.

Growing Up Grizzly

Grizzly bear cubs start life tiny and helpless, but they grow fast! Born during hibernation in the safety of their mother's den, cubs are blind, nearly hairless, and weigh only about 1 pound (0.5 kg). By the time the family emerges in spring, the cubs are already 10 to 20 pounds (4.5 to 9 kg) and full of curiosity.

At first, cubs stay very close to their mother, learning about the world one cautious step at a time. They quickly gain strength, practicing by wrestling, tumbling, and chasing each other—all playful behaviors that help them develop balance, muscle, and coordination. These skills are essential for climbing over logs, digging for food, and escaping danger.

Cubs nurse for several months, but they begin sampling solid food just weeks after leaving the den. They watch their mother closely, learning by imitation: how to dig, fish, sniff out berries, and even flip over rocks in search of insects. A grizzly cub's early years are full of learning and growing.

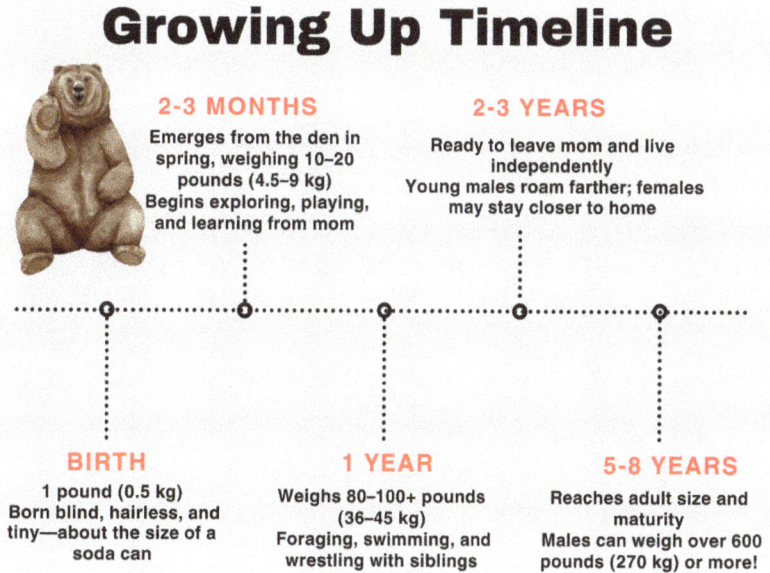

Growing Up Timeline

2-3 MONTHS
Emerges from the den in spring, weighing 10–20 pounds (4.5–9 kg)
Begins exploring, playing, and learning from mom

2-3 YEARS
Ready to leave mom and live independently
Young males roam farther; females may stay closer to home

BIRTH
1 pound (0.5 kg)
Born blind, hairless, and tiny—about the size of a soda can

1 YEAR
Weighs 80–100+ pounds (36–45 kg)
Foraging, swimming, and wrestling with siblings

5-8 YEARS
Reaches adult size and maturity
Males can weigh over 600 pounds (270 kg) or more!

Grizzly mothers are highly protective and patient teachers. Cubs follow her everywhere and rely on her for food, safety, and guidance. She leads them across rivers, through forests, and up steep slopes as they explore their home range together.

Cubs typically stay with their mother for 2 to 3 years, making this one of the longest childhoods among land mammals. During this time, they grow rapidly—gaining strength, independence, and the survival skills they'll need to live on their own.

When the time comes, the family begins to separate. Male cubs usually wander off first to begin solitary lives, while females may remain closer to their mother's range, sometimes overlapping with their siblings or offspring later in life.

Guardians of the Wilderness

Grizzly bears play several crucial roles in maintaining their ecosystems:

- **Forest Gardeners** – Grizzlies act as natural gardeners, digging up soil as they search for roots and bulbs. This turns over the soil, aerates it, and helps mix in nutrients. Their digging creates perfect spots for new plants to grow and flourish.

- **Seed Spreaders** – Grizzlies eat enormous amounts of berries and fruits, and their droppings contain seeds that they scatter across vast areas. Some seeds actually grow better after passing through a bear's digestive system! This helps forests regenerate and keeps plant communities diverse.

- **Salmon Transporters** – In coastal areas, grizzlies catch salmon from rivers and often carry them into the forest to eat. This moves important nutrients from the ocean to the land, fertilizing trees and plants up to 500 meters from streams. These nutrients help forests grow stronger and healthier.

- **Population Controllers** – By hunting young deer, elk, and moose, grizzlies help control these populations. This prevents overgrazing and helps maintain healthier prey populations by removing sick or weak individuals.

- **Habitat Creators** – Abandoned bear dens become homes for smaller animals, while areas where bears have dug extensively create unique microhabitats for specialized plants and small creatures. Their wallows can collect water, creating small wetland areas.

- **Balance Keepers** – As top predators, grizzlies influence the behavior and numbers of other predators like wolves and coyotes through competition. This creates a more balanced predator community and prevents any single predator species from becoming too dominant.

- **Ecosystem Health Indicators** – Because grizzlies need large, connected habitats with abundant food sources, their population health reflects the overall condition of their ecosystems. Thriving grizzly populations generally indicate healthy, functioning wilderness areas.

- **Keystone Species** – Grizzlies play a key role in maintaining balance in their habitats. Protecting grizzlies helps protect entire ecosystems, ensuring the survival of countless other species that depend on the same environment.

Grizzly bears do more than just live in their environment—they help shape and sustain it, making them one of the most important species in North American wilderness areas.

Natural Predators

Grizzly bears are apex predators, meaning they sit at the top of the food chain. Their massive size, incredible strength, and fierce defensive abilities make adult grizzlies nearly invulnerable to predation. However, they still face some threats, especially when they're young or weak.

- **Other Grizzlies** – The greatest threat to young grizzlies often comes from adult male bears. Large males sometimes kill cubs that aren't their own. This is one reason why mother bears are extremely protective and cautious.
- **Wolf Packs** – While wolves rarely attack adult grizzlies, a large pack might occasionally target a very young, old, or injured bear. More commonly, wolves and grizzlies compete for the same food sources and sometimes steal each other's kills.
- **Mountain Lions** – Like wolves, mountain lions generally avoid adult grizzlies but might opportunistically prey on a bear cub if it becomes separated from its mother.

Built for Dominance

As top predators, grizzlies have incredible features that make them nearly unbeatable in the wild:

- **Massive Size** – An adult male grizzly can weigh up to 800 pounds and stand over 8 feet tall on its hind legs, intimidating nearly any potential threat.
- **Powerful Claws** – A grizzly's 4-inch claws can deliver devastating blows to enemies. One swipe from a grizzly's paw can be fatal to even large animals.
- **Incredible Strength** – Grizzlies can flip boulders weighing hundreds of pounds and move fallen logs with ease. This strength makes them formidable opponents.
- **Keen Senses** – Their excellent sense of smell alerts them to danger from miles away, while their good hearing and decent vision help them stay aware of their surroundings.
- **Fierce Defense** – Mother bears with cubs are particularly dangerous, as they will fight to the death to protect their young. Even large predators know to avoid a mother grizzly with cubs.

While cubs may face some dangers, adult grizzlies have very few natural enemies. Their position at the top of the food chain is well-earned through their size, strength, and fierce defensive capabilities. With few predators to fear, grizzly bears can focus on finding food, raising cubs, and surviving harsh winters.

Challenges and Threats

Beyond natural predators, grizzly bears face several serious threats, most of which are connected to human activities:

- **Habitat Loss** – As forests and mountains are developed for towns, roads, ski resorts, and logging, grizzlies are losing the vast spaces they need to roam and find food. Many now live in isolated, fragmented habitats, making it harder to survive and find mates.
- **Human-Bear Conflicts** – As people build homes and businesses in bear country, conflicts increase. Bears attracted to garbage, bird feeders, pet food, or fruit trees may lose their fear of humans. These "food-conditioned" bears often get into trouble and sometimes have to be relocated or even euthanized.
- **Roads and Highways** – Roads cut through bear habitat, creating dangerous barriers. Many bears are killed each year in vehicle collisions. Roads also make it easier for people to access remote areas, bringing more human activity into bear country.
- **Climate Change** – Rising temperatures affect the foods bears depend on. Earlier spring thaws can create a mismatch between when bears emerge from hibernation and when their traditional foods are available. In some regions, droughts reduce berry production, while pine beetles kill the trees that produce nutritious pine nuts.
- **Food Source Reductions** – Some critical food sources for grizzlies are declining due to other factors. Salmon populations in many rivers have decreased due to dams, overfishing, and habitat degradation. With fewer high-calorie foods available, bears must work harder to prepare for hibernation.
- **Population Decline** – Once, about 50,000 grizzly bears roamed across the western United States. Today, only around 1,900 remain in the lower 48 states, occupying less than 2% of their historical range. While some populations are slowly recovering, grizzlies still face an uncertain future.

Conservation and Solutions

Efforts to protect grizzly bears include:

- Creating wildlife corridors to connect isolated populations
- Installing bear-proof garbage containers in communities near bear habitat
- Building wildlife crossings over highways to reduce collisions
- Educating people about safe practices in bear country
- Protecting salmon streams and other important food sources
- Restoring habitats damaged by development or resource extraction

By protecting grizzly bears, we help preserve North America's wilderness ecosystems and ensure these magnificent animals continue to roam the wild for generations to come.

Life Span and Population

Wild grizzly bears typically live 15-20 years on average. In protected environments like wildlife sanctuaries or zoos, grizzlies can live longer—sometimes up to 30 or even 35 years—thanks to regular veterinary care and a safe environment.

Female grizzlies generally live longer than males. This is partly because males engage in more risky behaviors like fighting for dominance and traveling across larger territories, which increases their chances of conflict with humans or other bears.

Grizzly bears once roamed across much of North America, from California to the Great Plains and even into northern Mexico. But as human populations expanded, grizzly numbers declined dramatically due to hunting, habitat loss, and other pressures.

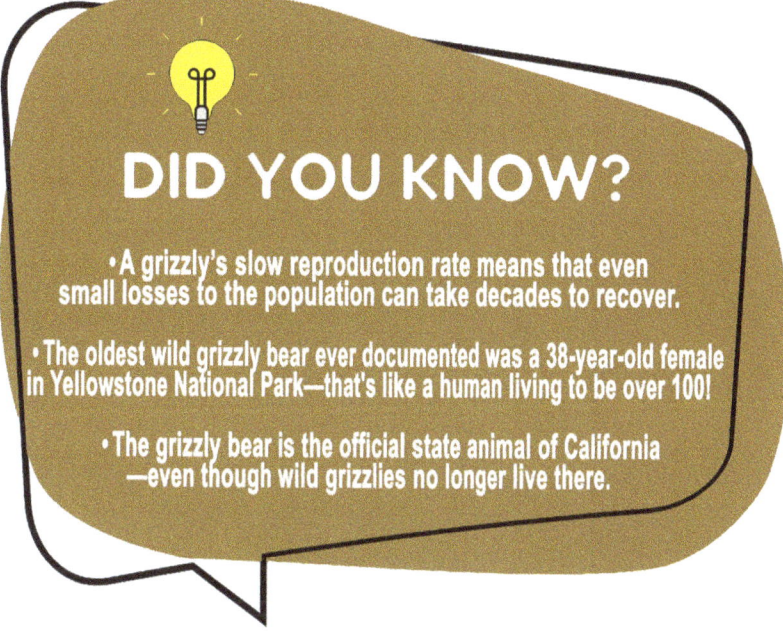

DID YOU KNOW?

- A grizzly's slow reproduction rate means that even small losses to the population can take decades to recover.
- The oldest wild grizzly bear ever documented was a 38-year-old female in Yellowstone National Park—that's like a human living to be over 100!
- The grizzly bear is the official state animal of California—even though wild grizzlies no longer live there.

Today, grizzly bears are considered a threatened species in the continental United States and are listed as "Least Concern" globally by the International Union for Conservation of Nature (IUCN), thanks to healthy populations in Alaska and Canada. However, local populations in the U.S. are still vulnerable.

Here's a snapshot of grizzly populations:

- **Alaska** – Home to the largest number of grizzlies, with an estimated 30,000 to 40,000 bears
- **Canada** – Approximately 20,000 to 25,000 grizzlies, mostly in British Columbia and Alberta
- **Lower 48 United States** – Only around 1,900 remain, mostly in Yellowstone, Glacier, and surrounding areas
- **Historical Range** – Grizzlies once lived in 17 U.S. states, but today are found in only 4 to 5

Altogether, there are an estimated 55,000 to 60,000 grizzly bears left in North America. Conservation efforts have helped some populations recover, especially in Yellowstone National Park, where the bear population has grown steadily since the 1970s. But challenges remain—especially in areas where bears come into conflict with roads, development, or livestock.

With continued protection, habitat conservation, and education, there is hope for a stable future for grizzlies across North America.

The Future for Grizzly Bears

Grizzly bears are among the most powerful and impressive animals in North America. Throughout this book, we've discovered what makes grizzlies such extraordinary creatures. From their remarkable adaptations to their critical role in ecosystems, grizzly bears show us how the natural world is connected in incredible ways.

Grizzlies are full of surprises. In addition to being powerful predators, they are also remarkably intelligent and adaptable. They can remember the locations of food sources for years, detect smells from miles away, and solve complex problems to find food. Their amazing physical strength—able to flip boulders weighing hundreds of pounds—is balanced by the gentle care they show their cubs over years of teaching and protection.

Even though grizzlies are strong, they face many challenges today. They're losing their homes as wilderness areas are developed, and conflicts with humans continue to threaten their survival. When we protect grizzlies, we also protect the forests, mountains, meadows, and rivers that many other animals need to survive.

Conservation efforts across North America have already made a difference. In places like Yellowstone and Glacier National Parks, grizzly populations are recovering, proving that when people come together to protect wildlife, real change is possible. Efforts like wildlife crossings, bear-proof containers, habitat protection, and community education offer hope for a future where grizzlies can continue to roam in wild places.

Seeing a grizzly bear in the wild is a powerful reminder of the wilderness we share with them—a world where every species plays a part in maintaining nature's delicate balance. By protecting grizzlies today, we ensure that future generations can experience the awe and wonder of these magnificent animals.

The story of grizzly bear conservation is far from over, but with continued dedication, we can help secure a future where these iconic symbols of wilderness not only survive but thrive in their natural habitats for generations to come.

Word Search

```
W U J E T A N R E B I H V Z F
N F E S R A E B G L B C W H O
O A T Y F S S E N R E D L I W
I K A S E T E R R I T O R Y W
T M M A C L L J R E M H A S I
A E I L O O L S H B D K J Y V
L T L M N O T O G A S P E W S
U S C O S P M X W A B T I N K
P Y L N E R J N L S A I O P S
O S C C R E Y A I R T I T W D
P O B U V D D V G V T O A A R
A C X B A A U I L A O L N L T
S E R S T T M V T Y C R J E K
S U R M I O R P D V U K E C E
P T L R O R A S L A M M A M A
R K M T N D X S O L I T A R Y
G J T D A D G Z W E V I Q Q M
S R Z E O T T S E N S E S P M
```

Adaptations	Ecosystem	Predator
Alaska	Habitat	Salmon
Bears	Hibernate	Senses
Claws	Mammals	Solitary
Climate	Migrate	Territory
Conservation	Omnivore	Wilderness
Cubs	Population	Yellowstone

Resources and References

- Alaska Department of Fish and Game. Brown Bear (Ursus arctos). adfg.alaska.gov, www.adfg.alaska.gov/index.cfm?adfg=brownbear.main. Accessed 25 Mar. 2025.

- Craighead, Frank C., Jr. Track of the Grizzly. Sierra Club Books, 1982.

- Garshelis, David L. "Grizzly Bear." Encyclopedia Britannica, 17 May 2023, www.britannica.com/animal/grizzly-bear. Accessed 24 Mar. 2025.

- International Union for Conservation of Nature (IUCN). Ursus arctos: The IUCN Red List of Threatened Species, www.iucnredlist.org/species/41688/145395786. Accessed 22 Mar. 2025.

- Kalman, Bobbie. Grizzly Bears. Crabtree Publishing Company, 2007.

- National Geographic Kids. Grizzly Bear Facts. kids.nationalgeographic.com, kids.nationalgeographic.com/animals/mammals/facts/grizzly-bear. Accessed 24 Mar. 2025.

- National Park Service. Grizzly Bears – Yellowstone National Park, nps.gov/yell/learn/nature/bears.htm. Accessed 20 Mar. 2025.

- Ransom, Candice F. Grizzly Bears. Children's Press, 2015.

- Servheen, Christopher, et al. Conservation Strategy for the Grizzly Bear in the Greater Yellowstone Ecosystem. U.S. Fish and Wildlife Service, 2016.

- Smith, Douglas W., and Gary Ferguson. Decade of the Wolf: Returning the Wild to Yellowstone. Lyons Press, 2005.

- U.S. Fish and Wildlife Service. Grizzly Bear Recovery Program, www.fws.gov/program/grizzly-bear-recovery. Accessed 21 Mar. 2025.

- Washington Department of Fish and Wildlife. Living with Grizzly Bears, wdfw.wa.gov/species-habitats/species/ursus-arctos. Accessed 23 Mar. 2025.

Published by Dylanna Press an imprint of Dylanna Publishing, Inc.
Copyright © 2025 by Dylanna Press
Author: Tyler Grady
All rights reserved. No part of this publication may be reproduced, stored in a retrieval system, or transmitted by any means, including electronic, mechanical, photocopying, or otherwise, without prior written permission of the publisher.

Although the publisher has taken all reasonable care in the preparation of this book, we make no warranty about the accuracy or completeness of its content and, to the maximum extent permitted, disclaim all liability arising from its use.

Printed in the U.S.A.

www.ingramcontent.com/pod-product-compliance
Lightning Source LLC
Chambersburg PA
CBHW040224040426
42333CB00051B/3446